Lean and Green Air Fryer Breakfast

A Complete Diet Recipes Collection for your Breakfast

Roxana Sutton

TABLE OF CONTENTS

Easy, Crispy, And Perfect Air Fryer Bacon

Cook Time: 10 minutes

Total Time: 10 minutes

Servings: 2

Ingredients

- 6 slices Bacon

Instructions

Line the air fryer basket with parchment paper. Parchment paper will soak up the grease and prevent the air fryer from smoking. Place the bacon on top of the paper. It's ok for the bacon to touch. I do not recommend stacking the bacon.

Some air fryer brands may need a trivet placed on top of the bacon. If you have an air fryer that is older or is very loud, you may need a trivet to hold the bacon down. I did not need this while using a Power Air Fryer.

Cook the bacon for 10 minutes at 380 degrees. I did not flip the bacon. Cook for additional time as necessary to reach your desired level of crunch.

Nutrition Facts

Calories: 75kcal | Protein: 6g | Fat: 6g

Air Fryer Bacon And Egg Bite Cups (Keto Low-Carb)

Prep Time: 10 Minutes

Cook Time: 15 Minutes

Total Time: 25 Minutes

Ingredients

- 6 large eggs
- 2 tablespoons of heavy whipping cream or milk (any is fine)
- Salt and pepper to taste
- ¼ cup chopped green peppers
- ¼ cup chopped red peppers
- ¼ cup chopped onions
- ¼ cup chopped fresh spinach
- ½ cup shredded cheddar cheese
- ¼ cup shredded mozzarella cheese
- 3 slices of cooked and crumbled bacon

Instructions

Add the eggs to a large mixing bowl.

Add in the cream, salt, and pepper to taste. Whisk to combine.

Sprinkle in the green peppers, red peppers, onions, spinach, cheeses, and bacon. I like to add only half of the ingredients here.

Whisk to combine.

I recommend you place the silicone molds in the air fryer before pouring in the egg mixture. This way you don't have to move the filled cups.

Pour the egg mixture into each of the silicone molds. I didn't need to spray mine and they didn't stick. If you have not used your molds yet, you may want to spray with cooking spray first to be sure.

Sprinkle in the remaining half of all of the veggies.

Cook the egg bites cups for 12-15 minutes at 300 degrees. You can test the center of one with a toothpick. When the toothpick comes out clean, the eggs have set.

Nutrition Information

Calories: 119|Total Fat: 9g|Carbohydrates: 2g|Protein: 8g

Quick And Easy Air Fryer Sausage

Cook Time: 20 Minutes

Total Time: 20 Minutes

Servings: 5

Ingredients

- 5 raw and uncooked sausage links

Instructions

Line the air fryer basket with parchment paper. Parchment paper will soak up the grease and prevent the air fryer from smoking. Place the sausage on top of the paper. It's ok for the sausages to touch.

Cook for 15 minutes at 360 degrees. Open and flip and cook an additional 5 minutes or until the sausage reaches an internal temperature of 160 degrees. Use a meat thermometer. You can also flip halfway through.

Cool before serving.

Nutrition Facts

Calories: 260kcal | Carbohydrates: 3g | Protein: 14g | Fat: 21g

Easy Air Fryer French Toast Sticks

Prep Time: 10 minutes

Cook Time: 12 minutes

Total Time: 22 minutes

Ingredients

- 4 slices Texas Toast bread I used Sarah Lee
- 1 tablespoon melted butter measured solid
- 1 egg beaten
- 2 tablespoons sweetener
- 1 teaspoon ground cinnamon
- 1/4 cup milk
- 1 teaspoon vanilla

Instructions

Cut each slice of bread into 3 strip pieces.

Add the beaten egg, sweetener, cinnamon, milk, and vanilla to the bowl with the melted butter. Stir to combine.

Spray the air fryer basket with cooking oil spray.

Dredge each piece of bread in the French toast batter. Be careful not to dredge each stick in too much batter. You may run out of batter if so.

Place the French toast sticks in the air fryer basket. Do not overcrowd. Spray with cooking oil.

Air Fry for 8 minutes at 370 degrees.

Open the air fryer and flip the French toast. Cook for an additional 2-4 minutes or until crisp.

Nutrition Facts

Calories: 52kcal | Carbohydrates: 7g | Protein: 2g | Fat: 2g

Paleo Crispy Air Fryer Sweet Potato Hash Browns

Prep Time: 10 minutes

Cook Time: 20 minutes

Soak in water: 20 minutes

Total Time: 50 minutes

Servings: 4

Ingredients

- 4 sweet potatoes peeled
- 2 garlic cloves minced
- 1 teaspoon cinnamon
- 1 teaspoon paprika salt and pepper to taste
- 2 teaspoons olive oil

Instructions

Grate the sweet potatoes using the largest holes of a cheese grater.

Place the sweet potatoes in a bowl of cold water. Allow the sweet potatoes to soak for 20-25 minutes. Soaking the sweet potatoes in cold water will help remove the starch from the potatoes. This makes them crunchy.

Drain the water from the potatoes and dry them completely using a paper towel.

Place the potatoes in a dry bowl. Add the olive oil, garlic, paprika, and salt and pepper to taste. Stir to combine the ingredients.

Add the potatoes to the air fryer. Cook for ten minutes at 400 degrees.

Open the air fryer and shake the potatoes. Cook for an additional ten minutes. Cool before serving.

Nutrition Facts

Calories: 134kcal

Easy Air Fryer Hard Boiled Eggs

Cook Time: 16 minutes

Cooling: 5 minutes

Total Time: 21 minutes

Ingredients

- 6 large eggs You can use whatever size eggs you want and however many you want that will fit in the air fryer basket without stacking.

Instructions

Place the eggs on the air fryer basket. Air fryer for 16 minutes at 260 degrees.

Open the air fryer and remove the eggs. Place them in a bowl with ice and cold water. Allow the eggs to cool for 5 minutes.

Peel and serve.

Nutrition Facts

Calories: 72kcal | Protein: 6g | Fat: 5g

Easy Air Fryer Cherry Turnovers

Prep Time: 15 minutes

Cook Time: 10 minutes

Total Time: 25 minutes

Ingredients

- 17 oz package puff pastry
- 4 sheets
- 10 oz can of cherry pie filling
- 1 egg beaten
- 2 tablespoons water ù
- cooking oil I use olive oil.

Instructions

Lay the pastry sheets on a flat surface.

Unfold both sheets of the puff pastry dough. Cut each sheet into 4 squares, making 8 squares total. Beat the egg in a small bowl along with the water to create an egg wash.

Use a cooking brush or your fingers to brush along the edges of each square with the egg wash.

Load 1 to 1 1/2 tablespoons of cherry pie filling into the middle of each s?uare sheet. Do not overfill the pastry.

Fold the dough over diagonally to create a triangle and seal the dough. Use the back of a fork to press lines into the open edges of each turnover to seal.

Make 3 slits into the top of the crust to vent the turnovers.

Brush the top of each turnover with the egg wash. (You can also do this step after you have placed them in the air fryer basket.)

Spritz the air fryer basket with cooking oil and add the turnovers. Make sure they do not touch and do not stack the turnovers. Cook in batches if needed.

Air fry at 370 degrees for 8 minutes. I did not flip.

Allow the pastries to cool for 2-3 minutes before removing them from the air fryer. This will ensure they do not stick.

Nutrition Facts

Calories: 224kcal | Carbohydrates: 27g | Protein: 4g | Fat: 12g

Air Fryer Blueberry Muffins

Prep Time: 10 minutes

Cook Time: 15 minutes

Total Time: 25 minutes

Ingredients

- 1 1/2 cups all-purpose or white whole wheat flour
- 3/4 cup old-fashioned oats (oatmeal)
- 1/2 cup brown sweetener. Light brown sugar can be used if preferred
- 1 tablespoon baking powder
- 1/2 teaspoon cinnamon
- 1/2 teaspoon salt
- 1 cup milk
- 1/4 cup melted unsalted butter (at room temperature)
- 2 eggs (at room temperature)
- 2 teaspoons vanilla
- 1 cup blueberries You can use fresh or frozen blueberries. If using frozen, do not thaw.

Instructions

Combine the flour, rolled oats, salt, cinnamon, brown sweetener, and baking powder in a large mixing bowl. Mix.

Combine the milk, eggs, vanilla, and butter in a separate medium-sized bowl. Mix using a silicone spoon.

Add the wet ingredients to the dry ingredients in the mixing bowl. Stir. Fold in the blueberries and stir.

Divide the batter among 12 silicone muffin cups and add them to the air fryer. Spraying the liners with oil is optional. The muffins generally don't stick.

Place the air fryer at 350 degrees. Monitor the muffins closely for proper cook time, as every model will cook differently. The muffins will need to cook for 11-15 minutes. Insert a toothpick into the middle of a muffin, if it returns clean the muffins have finished baking. Mine was ready at about 13 minutes.

Nutrition Facts

Calories: 121kcal | Carbohydrates: 13g | Protein: 3g | Fat: 5g

Air Fryer Loaded Hash Browns

Prep Time: 10 minutes

Cook Time: 20 minutes

Soak in water: 20 minutes

Total Time: 50 minutes

Ingredients

- 3 russet potatoes
- 1/4 cup chopped green peppers
- 1/4 cup chopped red peppers
- 1/4 cup chopped onions
- 2 garlic cloves chopped
- 1 teaspoon paprika
- salt and pepper to taste
- 2 teaspoons olive oil

Instructions

Grate the potatoes using the largest holes of a cheese grater.

Place the potatoes in a bowl of cold water. Allow the potatoes to soak for 20-25 minutes. Soaking the potatoes in cold water will help remove the starch from the potatoes. This makes them crunchy.

Drain the water from the potatoes and dry them completely using a paper towel.

Place the potatoes in a dry bowl. Add the garlic, paprika, olive oil, and salt and pepper to taste. Stir to combine the ingredients.

Add the potatoes to the air fryer. Cook for ten minutes at 400 degrees.

Open the air fryer and shake the potatoes.

Add the chopped peppers and onions. Cook for an additional ten minutes. Cool before serving.

Nutrition Facts

Calories: 246kcal | Carbohydrates: 42g | Protein: 6g | Fat: 3g

Air Fryer Homemade Strawberry Pop-Tarts

Prep Time: 15 minutes

Cook Time: 10 minutes

Total Time: 25 minutes

Ingredients

- 2 refrigerated pie crusts I used Pillsbury.
- 1 teaspoon cornstarch
- 1/3 cup low-sugar strawberry preserves I used Smucker's.
- Cooking oil I used olive oil.
- 1/2 cup plain, non-fat vanilla Greek yogurt
- 1 oz cream cheese I used reduced-fat.
- 1 tablespoon sweetener
- 1 teaspoon sugar sprinkles

Instructions

Lay the pie crust on a flat working surface. I used a bamboo cutting board.

Using a knife or pizza cutter, cut the 2 pie crusts into 6 rectangles (3 from each pie crust). Each should be fairly long as you will fold it over to close the pop tart.

Add the preserves and cornstarch to a bowl and mix well.

Add a tablespoon of the preserves to the crust. Place the preserves in the upper area of the crust. Fold each over to close the pop tarts.

Using a fork, make imprints in each of the pop tarts, to create vertical and horizontal lines along the edges.

Place the pop tarts in the Air Fryer. Do not stack, cook in batches if needed. Spray with cooking oil. Cook on 370 degrees for 10 minutes. You may want to check in on the Pop-Tarts for around 8 minutes to ensure they aren't too crisp for your liking.

Combine the Greek yogurt, cream cheese, and sweetener in a bowl to create the frosting.

Allow the Pop-Tarts to cool before removing them from the Air Fryer. This is important. If you do not allow them to cool, they may break.

Remove the pop tarts from the Air Fryer. Top each with the frosting. Sprinkle sugar sprinkles throughout.

Nutrition Facts

Calories: 274kcal | Carbohydrates: 32g | Protein: 3g | Fat: 14g

Quick And Easy Air Fryer Grilled Cheese

Prep Time: 5 minutes

Cook Time: 7 minutes

Total Time: 12 minutes

Ingredients

- 4 slices of bread I used 100% Whole Wheat
- 1 tablespoon butter melted
- 2 slices mild cheddar cheese
- 5-6 slices cooked bacon
- Optional 2 slices mozzarella cheese

Instructions

Heat the butter in the microwave for 10-15 seconds to soften. Spread the butter onto one side of each of the slices of bread.

Place a slice of buttered bread (butter side down) onto the air fryer basket.

Load the remaining ingredients in the following order: a slice of cheddar cheese, sliced cooked bacon, a slice of mozzarella cheese, and top with another slice of bread (butter side up).

If you have an air fryer that is very loud, you will likely need to use a layer rack or trivet to hold down the sandwich to keep it from flying. My Power Air Fryer does not need this, but my louder Black + Decker air fryer requires this to anchor the sandwich and keep it from flying around inside the air fryer. Cook for 4 minutes at 370 degrees.

Open the air fryer. Flip the sandwich. Cook for an additional 3 minutes.

 Remove and serve.

Nutrition Facts

Calories: 486kcal | Carbohydrates: 25g | Protein: 25g | Fat: 26g

Air Fryer Sweet Potato Hash

Prep Time: 10 minutes

Cook Time: 25 minutes

Total Time: 35 minutes

Ingredients

- 3 medium sweet potatoes Chopped into chunks about 1 inch thick.
- 1/2 cup diced white onions
- 3 slices bacon cooked and crumbled.
- 1/2 cup chopped green peppers
- 2 garlic cloves minced
- 1/3 cup diced celery
- 1 tablespoon olive oil
- 1 teaspoon Tony Chachere Lite Creole Seasoning
- 1/2 teaspoon paprika
- 1/2 teaspoon dried chives

Instructions

Combine the sweet potato chunks, onions, celery, green peppers, and garlic in a large bowl.

Drizzle the olive oil throughout and then sprinkle the Tony Chachere Lite Creole Seasoning and paprika. Stir and mix well to combine.

Add the sweet potato mix to the air fryer basket. Do not overcrowd the basket. Cook in batches if needed.

Air fry for 10 minutes at 400 degrees.

Open the air fryer and shake the basket. Air fry for an additional 2-7 minutes until the sweet potatoes are crisp on the outside and tender to touch when pierced with a fork.

Sprinkle the crumbled bacon and dried chives throughout.

Nutrition Facts

Calories: 167kcal | Carbohydrates: 19g | Protein: 4g | Fat: 7g

Easy Air Fryer Roasted Potatoes

Prep Time: 10 minutes

Cook Time: 15 minutes

Total Time: 25 minutes

Ingredients

- 2 russet potatoes peeled and sliced into large chunks.
- 1 teaspoon olive oil
- 2 sprigs of fresh rosemary, use 1 sprig if you prefer a hint of rosemary flavor.
- 2 minced garlic cloves
- 1/2 teaspoon onion powder
- salt and pepper to taste
- cooking oil I use olive oil.

Instructions

Drizzle the potatoes with olive oil and season with garlic, onion powder, salt, and pepper to taste.

Spray the air fryer basket with cooking oil.

Add the potatoes to the air fryer basket along with the thyme. Do not overfill the basket. Cook in batches if needed.

Air fry for 10 minutes at 400 degrees.

Open the air fryer and shake the basket. Air fry for an additional 2-7 minutes until the sweet potatoes are crisp on the outside and tender to touch when pierced with a fork.

Cool before serving.

Nutrition Facts

Calories: 68kcal | Carbohydrates: 13g | Protein: 2g | Fat: 1g

Air Fryer Cinnamon Sugar Donuts

Prep Time: 5 minutes

Cook Time: 16 minutes

Total Time: 21 minutes

Ingredients

- 8 oz can of biscuits
- 1 teaspoon ground cinnamon
- 1-2 teaspoons stevia
- 1/4 cup of table sugar can be substituted
- cooking oil spray I used avocado oil

Instructions

Lay the biscuits on a flat surface. Use a small circle cookie cutter or a biscuit cutter to cut holes in the middle of the biscuits. I used a protein powder scoop

Spray the air fryer basket with oil.

Place the donuts in the air fryer. Spray the donuts with oil. Do not stack the donuts. Cook in two batches if needed.

Cook for 4 minutes at 360 degrees.

Open the air fryer and flip the donuts. Cook for an additional 4 minutes. Repeat for the remaining donuts.

Spritz the donuts with additional oil.

Add the cinnamon and sugar to separate bowls. Dip the donuts in the cinnamon and sugar. Serve!

Nutrition Facts

Calories: 186kcal | Carbohydrates: 25g | Protein: 3g | Fat: 9g

Air Fryer Fried Pork Chops Southern Style

Prep Time: 5 minutes

Cook Time: 20 minutes

Optional marinate: 30 minutes

Total Time: 25 minutes

Ingredients

- 4 pork chops (bone-in or boneless)
- 3 tbsp buttermilk I used fat-free
- 1/4 cup all-purpose flour
- Seasoning Salt to taste You can also use either a chicken or pork rub.
- pepper to taste
- 1 Ziploc bag cooking oil spray

Instructions

Pat the pork chops dry.

Season the pork chops with the seasoning salt and pepper. Drizzle the buttermilk over the pork chops.

Place the pork chops in a Ziploc bag with the flour. Shake to fully coat.

Marinate for 30 minutes. This step is optional. This helps the flour adhere to the pork chops. Place the pork chops in the air fryer. I do not recommend you stack. Cook in batches if necessary. Spray the pork chops with cooking oil.

Cook the pork chops for 15 minutes at 380 degrees. Flip the pork chops over to the other side after 10 minutes.

Nutritional Facts

Calories: 173kcal | Carbohydrates: 7g | Protein: 22g | Fat: 6g

Ninja Foodi Low-Carb Breakfast Casserole {Air Fryer}

Prep Time: 10 Minutes

Cook Time: 15 Minutes

Total Time: 25 Minutes

Ingredients

- 1 LB Ground Sausage
- 1/4 Cup Diced White Onion
- 1 Diced Green Bell Pepper
- 8 Whole Eggs, Beaten
- 1/2 Cup Shredded Colby Jack Cheese
- 1 Tsp Fennel Seed
- 1/2 Tsp Garlic Salt

Instructions

If you are using the Ninja Foodi, use the saute function to brown the sausage in the pot of the food. If you are using an air fryer, you can use a skillet to do this.

Add in the onion and pepper and cook along with the ground sausage until the veggies are soft and the sausage is cooked.

Using the 8.75-inch pan or the Air Fryer pan, spray it with non-stick cooking spray. Place the ground sausage mixture on the bottom of the pan.

Top evenly with cheese.

Pour the beaten eggs evenly over the cheese and sausage. Add fennel seed and garlic salt evenly over the eggs.

Place the rack in the low position in the Ninja Foodi, and then place the pan on top. Set to Air Crisp for 15 minutes at 390 degrees.

If you are using an air fryer, place the dish directly into the basket of the air fryer and cook for 15 minutes at 390 degrees.

Carefully remove and serve.

Nutrition Information

Calories:282|Totalfat:23g|Saturatedfat:8g|Transfat:12g|Cholesterol:227mg|Sodium: 682mg|Carbohydrates: 3g|Sugar: 2g|Protein: 15g

Air Fryer Donuts

Prep Time: 10 Mins

Cook Time: 5 Mins

Total Time: 15 Mins

Ingredients

- 16 oz refrigerated flaky jumbo biscuits
- 1/2 c. Granulated white sugar
- 2 tsp ground cinnamon
- 4 tbsp butter melted
- Olive or coconut oil spray

Instructions

Combine sugar and cinnamon in a shallow bowl; set aside.

Remove the biscuits from the can, separate them and place them on a flat surface. Use a 1-inch round biscuit cutter (or similarly-sized bottle cap) to cut holes out of the center of each biscuit.

Lightly coat the air fryer basket with olive or coconut oil spray. Do not use a non-stick spray like Pam because it can damage the coating on the basket.

Place 4 donuts in a single layer in the air fryer basket. Make sure they are not touching. Air Fry at 360 degrees F for 5 minutes or until lightly browned.

Remove donuts from Air Fryer, dip in melted butter then roll in cinnamon sugar to coat. Serve immediately.

Nutrition Facts

Calories: 316kcal Carbohydrates: 42g Protein: 3g

Fat: 15g Saturated Fat: 5g

Cholesterol: 15mg Sodium: 585mg Potassium: 127mg Fiber: 1g

Sugar: 16g Vitamin A: 175IU Calcium: 36mg Iron: 1.9mg

Air Fryer Breakfast Sausage

Prep Time: 10 Minutes

Cook Time: 10 Minutes

Total Time: 20 Minutes

Ingredients

- 1 lb ground pork 1 lb ground turkey
- 2 tsp fennel seeds
- 2 tsp dry rubbed sage
- 2 tsp garlic powder
- 1 tsp paprika
- 1 tsp sea salt
- 1 tsp dried thyme
- 1 tbsp real maple syrup

Instructions

Begin by mixing the pork and turkey in a large bowl. In a small bowl, mix the remaining ingredients: fennel, sage, garlic powder, paprika, salt, and thyme. Pour spices into the meat and continue to mix until the spices are completely incorporated.

Spoon into balls (about 2-3 tbsp of meat), and flatten into patties. Place inside the air fryer, you will probably have to do this in 2 batches.

Set the temperature to 370 degrees, and cook for 10 minutes. Remove from the air fryer and repeat with the remaining sausage.

Nutritional Value

Calories: 68kcal Carbohydrates: 13g Protein: 2g

Fat: 1g Sodium: 400g

Crispy Bacon In The Air Fryer

Cook Time: 10 Minutes

Total Time: 10 Minutes

Ingredients

- 1 Pound of Bacon

Instructions

Add bacon into the air fryer basket, evenly. This may take 2 batches to cook all of the bacon, depending on size.

Cook at 350 degrees for 5 minutes.

Turn bacon and cook an additional 5 minutes or until your desired crispiness. Remove bacon with tongs and place on a paper towel-lined plate.

Let cool and serve.

Nutrition Information

Calories:177|Totalfat:33g|Saturatedfat:5g|Transfat:0g|Cholesterol:37mg|Sodium: 637mg|Carbohydrates: 1g|Sugar: 0g|Protein: 13g

Air Fryer Breakfast Stuffed Peppers

Prep Time: 5 minutes

Cook Time: 13 minutes

Total Time: 18 minutes

Servings: 2

Ingredients

- 1 bell pepper halved, middle seeds removed
- 4 eggs
- 1 tsp olive oil
- 1 pinch salt and pepper
- 1 pinch sriracha flakes for a bit of spice, optional

Instructions

Cut bell peppers in half lengthwise and remove seeds and middle leaving the edges intact like bowls. Use your finger to rub a bit of olive oil just on the exposed edges (where it was cut).

Crack two eggs into each bell pepper half. Sprinkle with desired spices.

Set them on a trivet inside your Ninja Foodi or directly inside your other brand of the air fryer. Close the lid on your air fryer (the one attached to the Ninja Foodi machine).

Turn the machine on, press the air crisper button at 390 degrees for 13 minutes (times will vary slightly according to how well done you like your egg but this was perfect for us).

Alternatively, if you'd rather have your bell pepper and eggless brown on the outside add just one egg to your pepper and set the air fryer to 330 degrees for 15 minutes. (for an over hard egg consistency)

Nutrition Facts

Fat: 10g Saturated Fat: 3g

Cholesterol: 327mg Sodium: 146mg Potassium: 246mg
Carbohydrates: 4g Fiber: 1g

Sugar: 2g Protein: 11g Vitamin C: 76mg Calcium: 49mg Iron: 1.8mg

Air Fryer Bacon and Egg Breakfast Biscuit Bombs

Prep Time: 35 Mins

Cook Time: 15 Mins

Total: 50 MIN

Ingredients

- Biscuit Bombs
- 4 slices bacon, cut into 1/2-inch pieces
- 1 tablespoon butter
- 2 eggs, beaten
- 1/4 teaspoon pepper
- 1 can (10.2 oz) Pillsbury Grands! Southern Homestyle refrigerated
- Buttermilk biscuits (5 biscuits)
- 2 oz sharp cheddar cheese, cut into ten
- 3/4-inch cubes
- Egg Wash 1 egg
- 1 tablespoon water

Instruction

Prevent your screen from going dark while you cook.

Cut two 8-inch rounds of cooking parchment paper. Place one round at bottom of the air fryer basket. Spray with cooking spray.

In 10-inch nonstick skillet, cook bacon over medium-high heat until crisp. Remove from pan; place on paper towel. Carefully wipe skillet with a paper towel. Add butter to skillet; melt over medium heat. Add 2 beaten eggs and pepper to skillet; cook until eggs are thickened but still moist, stirring fre?uently. Remove from heat; stir in bacon. Cool 5 minutes.

Meanwhile, separate dough into 5 biscuits; separate each biscuit into 2 layers. Press each into a 4-inch round. Spoon 1 heaping tablespoonful of egg mixture onto the center of each round. Top with one piece of cheese. Gently fold edges up and over filling; pinch to seal. In a small bowl, beat the remaining egg and water. Brush biscuits on all sides with egg wash.

Place 5 of the biscuit bombs, seam sides down, on parchment in the air fryer basket. Spray both sides of the second parchment round with cooking spray. Top biscuit bombs in a basket with a second parchment round, then top with remaining 5 biscuit bombs.

Set to 325°F; cook 8 minutes. Remove top parchment round; using tongs, carefully turn biscuits, and place in basket in a single layer. Cook 4 to 6 minutes longer or until cooked through (at least 165°F).

Nutrition Information

Calories: 200 Total Fat: 12g Saturated Fat: 6g Cholesterol: 85mg Sodium: 440mg Potassium: 50mg

Total Carbohydrate: 17g Sugars: 3g

Protein: 7g

Air Fryer Sausage Breakfast Casserole

Prep Time: 10 Minutes

Cook Time: 20 Minutes

Total Time: 30 Minutes

Ingredients

- 1 Lb Hash Browns
- 1 Lb Ground Breakfast Sausage
- 1 Green Bell Pepper Diced
- 1 Red Bell Pepper Diced
- 1 Yellow Bell Pepper Diced
- 1/4 Cup Sweet Onion Diced
- 4 Eggs

Instructions

Foil line the basket of your air fryer. Place the hash browns on the bottom. Top it with the uncooked sausage.

Evenly place the peppers and onions on top. Cook on 355* for 10 minutes.

Open the air fryer and mix up the casserole a bit if needed. Crack each egg in a bowl, then pour right on top of the casserole. Cook on 355* for another 10 minutes.

Serve with salt and pepper to taste.

Nutrition Information

Calories:517|Totalfat:37g|Saturatedfat:10g|Transfat:0g|Cholesterol:227mg|Sodium: 1092mg|Carbohydrates:27g|Sugar: 4g|Protein: 21g

Air Fryer Baked Egg Cups w/ Spinach & Cheese

Prep Time: 5 mins

Cook Time: 10 mins

Total Time: 15 mins

Ingredients

- 1 large egg
- 1 tablespoon (15 ml) milk or half & half
- 1 tablespoon (15 ml) frozen spinach, thawed (or sautéed fresh spinach)
- 1-2 teaspoons (5 ml) grated cheese
- Salt, to taste
- Black pepper, to taste
- Cooking spray, for muffin cups or ramekins

Instructions

Spray inside of silicone muffin cups or ramekin with oil spray. Add egg, milk, spinach, and cheese into the muffin cup or ramekin.

Season with salt and pepper. Gently stir ingredients into egg whites without breaking the yolk.

Air Fry at 330°F for about 6-12 minutes (single egg cups usually take about 6 minutes - multiple or doubled up cups take as much as 12. As you add more egg cups, you will need to add more time.) Cooking in a ceramic ramekin may take a little longer. If you want runny yolks, cook for less time. Keep checking the eggs after 5 minutes to ensure the egg is to your preferred texture.

Nutrition Facts

Calories: 115kcal | Carbohydrates: 1g | Protein: 10g | Fat: 7g | Saturated Fat: 2g | Cholesterol: 216mg | Sodium: 173mg | Potassium: 129mg | Sugar: 1g | Vitamin A: 2040IU | Calcium: 123mg | Iron: 1.3mg

Airfryer French Toast Sticks Recipe

Prep Time: 5 minutes

Cook Time: 12 minutes

Total Time: 17 minutes

Ingredients

- 4 pieces bread (whatever kind and thickness desired)
- 2 Tbsp butter (or margarine, softened)
- 2 eggs (gently beaten)
- 1 pinch salt
- 1 pinch cinnamon
- 1 pinch nutmeg
- 1 pinch ground cloves
- 1 tsp icing sugar (and/or maple syrup for garnish and serving)

Instructions

Preheat Airfryer to 180* Celsius.

In a bowl, gently beat together two eggs, a sprinkle of salt, a few heavy shakes of cinnamon, and small pinches of both nutmeg and ground cloves.

Butter both sides of bread slices and cut into strips.

Dredge each strip in the egg mixture and arrange it in Airfryer (you will have to cook in two batches). After 2 minutes of cooking, pause the Airfryer, take out the pan, making sure you place the pan on a heat-safe surface and spray the bread with cooking spray.

Once you have generously coated the strips, flip and spray the second side as well.

Return pan to the fryer and cook for 4 more minutes, checking after a couple of minutes to ensure they are cooking evenly and not burning.

When the egg is cooked and the bread is golden brown, remove it from Airfryer and serve immediately. To garnish and serve, sprinkle with icing sugar, top with whip cream, drizzle with maple syrup, or serve with a small bowl of syrup for dipping.

Nutrition Facts

Calories:178Kcal|Totalfat:15g|Saturatedfat:8g|Transfat:12g|Cholesterol:194mg|Sodium: 193mg|Carbohydrates: 2g|Sugar: 1g|Protein: 5g| Iron: 0.8mg| Calcium: 25mg

Air Fryer Breakfast Frittata

Prep Time: 15 mins Cook Time: 20 mins

Total Time: 35 mins

Ingredients

- ¼ pound breakfast sausage fully cooked and crumbled
- 4 eggs, lightly beaten
- ½ cup shredded Cheddar-Monterey Jack cheese blend
- 2 tablespoons red bell pepper, diced
- 1 green onion, chopped
- 1 pinch cayenne pepper (Optional) cooking spray

Direction

Combine sausage, eggs, Cheddar-Monterey Jack cheese, bell pepper. onion, and cayenne in a bowl and mix to combine.

Preheat the air fryer to 360 degrees F (180 degrees C). Spray a nonstick 6x2-inch cake pan with cooking spray.

Place egg mixture in the prepared cake pan.

Cook in the air fryer until frittata is set, 18 to 20 minutes.

Nutrition Facts

Calories: 380| Protein 31.2g| Carbohydrates 2.9g| Fat 27.4g| Cholesterol 443mg| Sodium 693.5mg| Vitamin A Iu: 894.6IU|Vitamin B6: 0.3mg|Vitamin C: 13.4mg|Calcium:69.2mg|Iron:3mg|Magnesium:26.7mg|Potassium:328.4mg| Sodium: 693.5mg|Thiamin: 0.1mg

Breakfast Potatoes In The Air Fryer

Prep Time: 2 minutes

Cook Time: 15 minutes

Total Time: 17 minutes

Servings: 2

Ingredients

- 5 medium potatoes, peeled and cut to 1-inch cubes (Yukon Gold works best)
- 1 tbsp oil
- Breakfast Potato Seasoning
- 1/2 tsp kosher salt
- 1/2 tsp smoked paprika
- 1/2 tsp garlic powder
- 1/4 tsp black ground pepper

Instructions

Preheat the air fryer for about 2-3 minutes at 400F degrees. This will give you the crispiest potatoes. Meanwhile, toss the potatoes with breakfast potato seasoning and oil until thoroughly coated.

Spray the air fryer basket with a nonstick spray. Add the potatoes and cook for about 15 minutes, stopping and shaking the basket 2-3 times throughout to promote even cooking.

Transfer to a plate and serve right away.

Nutrition Facts

Calories: 375 Fat: 7g Sodium: 635mg

Potassium: 2199mg63 Carbohydrates: 67g Fiber: 13

Protein: 13g Vitamin A: 245IU Vitamin: C 60.7mg Calcium: 160mg Iron: 17.4mg

Air-Fried Breakfast Bombs Are A Portable Healthy Meal

Active Time: 20 Mins

Total Time: 25 Mins

Yield: Serves 2

Ingredients

- 3 center-cut bacon slices
- 3 large eggs, lightly beaten
- 1 ounce 1/3-less-fat cream cheese, softened
- 1 tablespoon chopped fresh chives
- 4 ounces fresh prepared whole-wheat pizza dough
- Cooking spray

How To Make It

Step 1

Cook bacon in a medium skillet over medium until very crisp, about 10 minutes. Remove bacon from pan; crumble. Add eggs to bacon drippings in pan; cook, stirring often, until almost set but still loose, about 1 minute. Transfer eggs to a bowl; stir in cream cheese, chives, and crumbled bacon.

Step 2

Divide dough into 4 equal pieces. Roll each piece on a lightly floured surface into a 5-inch circle. Place one-fourth of the egg mixture in the center of each dough circle. Brush outside edge of dough with water; wrap dough around egg mixture to form a purse, pinching together dough at the seams.

Step 3

Place dough purses in a single layer in an air fryer basket; coat well with cooking spray. Cook at 350°F until golden brown, 5 to 6 minutes, checking after 4 minutes.

Nutritional Information

Calories: 305 Fat: 15g

Sat fat: 5g Unsatfat: 8g Protein: 19g Carbohydrate: 26g Fiber: 2g

Sugars: 1g Added sugars: 0g Sodium: 548mg

Air Fryer Scrambled Eggs

Prep Time: 3 Minutes

Cook Time: 9 Minutes

Total Time: 12 Minutes

Ingredients

- 1/3 tablespoon unsalted butter
- 2 eggs
- 2 tablespoons milk
- Salt and pepper to taste

- 1/8 cup cheddar cheese

Instructions

Place butter in an oven/air fryer-safe pan and place inside the air fryer. Cook at 300 degrees until butter is melted, about 2 minutes.

Whisk together the eggs and milk, then add salt and pepper to taste.

Place eggs in a pan and cook it at 300 degrees for 3 minutes, then push eggs to the inside of the pan to stir them around.

Cook for 2 more minutes then add cheddar cheese, stirring the eggs again. Cook 2 more minutes.

Remove pan from the air fryer and enjoy them immediately.

Nutrition Information

Calories:126Kcal|Totalfat:9g|Saturatedfat:4g|Transfat:0g|Cholesterol200mg|Sodium: 275mg|Carbohydrates: 1g|Sugar: 1g|Protein: 9g| Iron: 0.8mg| Calcium: 4mg

Air Fryer Banana Bread

Prep Time: 10 minutes

Cook Time: 28 minutes

Total Time: 38 minutes

Servings: 8

Ingredients

- 3/4 c all-purpose flour
- 1/4 tsp baking soda
- 1/4 tsp salt
- 1 egg
- 2 bananas overripe, mashed
- 1/2 tsp vanilla
- 1/4 c sour cream
- 1/4 c vegetable oil
- 1/2 c sugar
- 7" bundt pan

Instructions

Mix dry ingredients in one bowl and wet in another. Slowly combine the two until flour is incorporated, do not overmix.

Spray inside of 7" bundt pan with nonstick spray and pour in batter. Place inside air fryer basket and close. Set to 310 degrees for 28 minutes.

Remove when done and allow to sit in the pan for 5 minutes. Then gently flip over on a plate. Drizzle melted frosting on the top, slice, and serve.

Nutrition Facts

Calories: 198 Fat: 9g

Saturated Fat: 7g Cholesterol: 24mg Sodium: 121mg Potassium: 136mg Carbohydrates: 28g Fiber: 1g

Sugar: 16g Protein 2g Vitamin A: 93IU Vitamin C: 3mg Calcium: 14mg Iron: 1mg

Easy Air Fryer Breakfast Frittata

Prep Time: 5 min

Cook Time: 10 min

Total Time: 15 minutes

Yield: 4 servings

Ingredients

- 4 eggs
- ½ cup shredded sharp cheddar cheese
- ¼ cup fresh spinach, chopped
- 2 scallions, chopped
- 2 tablespoons half and half salt and pepper to taste

Instructions

In a medium bowl, beat eggs with half and half. Stir in cheese, spinach, scallions, salt, and pepper.

Spray a 6″ cake pan with cooking spray (very important). Pour mixture into the pan.

Air fry at 350 degrees (F) for 10-14 minutes. A toothpick inserted will come out clean when done. Let cool for 5 minutes before removing from pan and serving.

Nutritional Value

Calories:178Kcal|Totalfat:15g|Saturatedfat:8g|Transfat:12g|Cholesterol:194mg|Sodium: 193mg|Carbohydrates: 2g|Sugar: 1g|Protein: 5g| Iron: 0.8mg| Calcium: 25mg

Air Fryer Breakfast Pizza

Prep Time: 5 Minutes

Cook Time: 15 Minutes

Total Time: 20 Minutes

Ingredients

- Crescent Dough 3
- scrambled eggs crumbled sausage
- 1/2 chopped pepper
- 1/2 cup cheddar cheese
- 1/2 cup mozzarella cheese

Instructions

Spray Pan with oil,

Spread dough in the bottom of a Fat daddio or springform pan

Place in the air fryer on 350 for 5 minutes or until the top is slightly brown Remove from the air fryer

Top with Eggs, sausage, peppers, and cheese, Or use your favorite toppings.

Place in the air fryer for an additional 5-10 minutes or until the top is golden brown.

Nutrition Information

Calories:250Kcal|Totalfat:19g|Saturatedfat:9g|Transfat:0g|Cholesterol:167mg|Sodium: 193mg|Carbohydrates: 2g|Sugar: 2g|Protein: 14g| Iron: 1mg| Calcium: 13mg

Air Fryer Breakfast Sweet Potato Skins

Prep Time: 7 Minutes

Cook Time: 23 Minutes

Total Time: 30 Minutes

Ingredients

- 2 medium sweet potatoes
- 2 tsp. olive oil
- 4 eggs
- 1/4 c. whole milk salt and pepper
- 4 slices cooked bacon
- 2 green onions, sliced

Instructions

Wash the sweet potatoes and add 3-4 cuts to the potatoes. Microwave for 6-8 minutes, depending on their size until they are soft.

Using an oven mitt, slice the potatoes in half lengthwise. Scoop out the potato flesh, leaving 1/4 inch around the edges. Save the scooped sweet potato for another use.

Brush the potato skins with olive oil and sprinkle with sea salt. Arrange the skins in your Air Fryer basket and cook at 400° (or the highest available temp) for 10 minutes.

Meanwhile, add the eggs, milk, salt, and pepper to a non-stick skillet. Cook the mixture over medium heat, stirring constantly, until there are no longer any visible liquid eggs.

Top each cooked potato skin with 1/4 of the scrambled eggs and 1 slice of crumbled bacon. Cover with shredded cheese and cook for 3 minutes, or until the cheese is melted.

Serve topped with green onion.

Nutritional Value

Calories:208Kcal|Totalfat:12g|Saturatedfat:4g|Transfat:0g|Cholesterol:199mg|Sodium: 367mg|Carbohydrates: 14g|Sugar: 5g|Protein: 12g| Iron: 2mg|

Air Fryer French Toast Sticks

Prep Time: 7 Minutes

Cook Time: 8 Minutes

Total Time: 15 Minutes

Ingredients

- 12 slices Texas Toast
- 1 cup milk
- 5 large eggs
- 4 tbsp. butter, melted
- 1 tsp. vanilla extract
- 1/4 cup granulated sugar
- 1 tbsp. cinnamon Maple syrup, optional

Instructions

Slice each bread slice into thirds.

In a bowl, add the milk, eggs, butter, and vanilla. Whisk until combined. In a separate bowl, add the cinnamon and sugar.

Dip each breadstick quickly into the egg mixture. Sprinkle the sugar mixture onto both sides.

Place into the air fryer basket and cook at 350°F for about 8 minutes or until just crispy. Remove from basket and allow to cool. Serve with maple syrup, if desired.

Nutrition Information

Calories: 170| Total Fat: 8g| Saturated Fat: 4g| Cholesterol: 90mg| Sodium: 183mg| Fiber: 1g| Sugar: 7g| Protein: 6g

Air Fryer Breakfast Ta□uitos Recipe

Prep Time: 25 mins

Cook Time: 6 mins

Total Time: 31 mins

Ingredients

- pound ground turkey sausage
- 2 teaspoons onion powder
- 2 cloves garlic minced
- ½ teaspoon salt
- ½ teaspoon pepper
- 6 large eggs
- 16 small low carb flour or whole wheat tortillas
- 1 cup fat-free shredded Mexican blend or cheddar cheese
- 2 tablespoons I Can't Believe It's Not Butter Melted

Instructions

Preheat oven to 400 F degrees. Lightly spray a 9x13 baking dish with coconut oil

In a large skillet, cook sausage until it's is no longer pink. Drain. Add garlic and cook until soft. Season with onion powder, salt, and pepper.

In a bowl, whisk eggs and pour into the skillet and cook until eggs are scrambled. Remove skillet from the stovetop. Add mixture to a bowl and set aside.

Add tortillas to the microwave for 20 seconds. This softens them and makes it easier to roll them. On a flat surface, top a tortilla with 2 tablespoons of the skillet mixture. Top with a sprinkle of cheese. Roll the tortilla tightly and place in the baking dish. Brush with melted butter. Repeat until the remaining tortillas are filled.

Pre-heat Air Fryer to 350° for 1 minute. Bake for 3 minutes and turn, and bake for an additional 2-3 minutes or until tortillas are golden brown and crispy.

Serve with your favorite toppings!

Nutritional Facts

Calories:178Kcal|Totalfat:15g|Saturatedfat:8g|Transfat:12g|Cholesterol:194mg|Sodium: 193mg|Carbohydrates: 2g|Sugar: 1g|Protein: 5g| Iron: 0.8mg| Calcium: 25mg

Air Fryer French Toast

Prep Time: 5 mins

Cook Time: 9 mins

Total Time: 14 mins

Ingredients

- 2 eggs
- 2 TBS milk, cream, or half and half
- 1/2 tsp ground cinnamon
- 1/2 tsp vanilla extract
- 1 loaf challah or brioche bread, cut into 8 thick slices

Instructions

In a medium bowl, add egg, milk, vanilla, and cinnamon; whisk to combine completely; set aside Make an assembly line: set up whisked egg mixture and bread next to each other.

Spray the air fryer basket with nonstick oil spray

Dip the slices of bread into the egg mixture being sure to flip and coat both sides. Lift out of the mixture and allow to drip for a few seconds, then place into the air fryer basket. Repeat for remaining slices

Close the Air Fryer. Set to 400 degrees and 5 minutes. After 5 minutes, open the basket and carefully flip the french toast slices. Close the air fryer and cook for 3-4 more minutes at 400 degrees. *Time may vary slightly depending on the air fryer model.

Remove the french toast when finished and then cook the remaining french toast slices. Serve with warm maple syrup and powdered sugar or your favorite toppings!

Nutritional Value

Calories:150Kcal|Totalfat:12g|Saturatedfat:4g|Transfat:0g|Cholesterol:160mg|Sodium: 200mg|Carbohydrates: 4g|Sugar: 1g|Protein: 3g| Iron: 2mg|

Air Fryer Breakfast Pockets

Prep Time: 30 minutes

Cook Time: 15 minutes

Ingredients

- 1 lb of ground pork
- 4 whole eggs
- 1 whole egg for egg wash
- 1/3 + 1/4 c of whole milk
- 1-2 ounces of Velveeta cheese
- Salt and pepper to taste
- 2 packages of Pillsbury pie crust 2 crusts to a package
- 2-gallon ziplock bags
- parchment paper
- Cooking spray

Instructions

Remove pie crusts from the refrigerator. Brown and drain the pork.

Heat 1/4 c milk and cheese in a small pot until melted.

Whisk 4 eggs, season with salt and pepper, and add remaining milk. Scramble eggs in a skillet until almost fully cooked.

Mix the meat, cheese, and eggs.

Roll out your pie crust and cut it into a 3-4 inch circle (about the size of a cereal bowl). Whisk one egg to make an egg wash.

Place about 2 tbsps of mix into the middle of each circle.

Egg wash all edges of the circle.

Fold the circle creating a moon shape. Crimp the folded edges with a fork.

Layer the pockets in parchment paper and place them in a plastic ziplock bag overnight. Once ready to cook, pre-heat your Air Fryer to 360 degrees.

Spray each side of the pocket with cooking spray.

Place pockets in pre-heated Air Fryer for 15 minutes or until golden brown. Remove from Air Fryer and allow to cool for a few minutes before serving.

Nutritional Value

Calories:140Kcal|Totalfat:15g|Saturatedfat:8g|Transfat:2g|Cholesterol:160mg|Sodium: 180mg|Carbohydrates: 2g|Sugar:2g|Protein: 10g| Iron: 2mg| Calcium: 13mg

Air Fryer Cheesy Baked Eggs

Prep Time: 4 minutes

Cook Time: 16 minutes

Total Time: 20 minutes

Servings: 2

Ingredients

- 4 large Eggs
- 2 ounces Smoked gouda, chopped
- Everything bagel seasoning
- Salt and pepper to taste

Instructions

Spray the inside of each ramekin with cooking spray. Add 2 eggs to each ramekin, then add 1 ounce of chopped gouda to each. Salt and pepper to taste. Sprinkle your everything bagel seasoning on top of each ramekin (as much as you like). Place each ramekin into the air fryer basket. Cook for 400F for 16 minutes, or until eggs are cooked through. Serve.

Nutrition

Calories: 240kcal | Carbohydrates: 1g | Protein: 12g | Fat: 16g

Low-Carb Air Fryer Bacon And Egg Cups

Prep Time: 10 Minutes

Cook Time: 10 Minutes

Total Time: 20 Minutes

Ingredients

- 3 slices bacon, sliced in half
- 6 large eggs
- 1 bunch green onions, optional salt and pepper, optional

Instructions

Arrange 6 baking cups (silicone or paper) in the air fryer basket. Spray with nonstick cooking spray. Line cups with bacon slice. Carefully crack an egg into each cup. Season with salt and pepper, if desired.

Turn the air fryer on to 330° and cook for 10 minutes, until eggs are set. Carefully remove from air fryer and garnish with desired toppings.

Nutrition Information

Calories:115Kcal|Totalfat:9g|Saturatedfat:3g|Transfat:0g|Cholesterol:10mg|Sodium: 160mg|Carbohydrates: 0g|Sugar: 0g|Protein: 8g| Iron: 2mg|

Air Fryer English Breakfast

Prep Time: 3 mins

Cook Time: 15 mins

Total Time:18 mins

Ingredients

- 6 English Sausages
- 6 Bacon Rashers
- 2 Large Tomatoes
- 4 Black Pudding
- ½ Can Baked Beans
- 2 Large Eggs
- 1 Tbsp Whole Milk
- 1 Tsp Butter
- Salt & Pepper

Instructions

Crack your eggs into a ramekin and stir in butter, milk, and salt and pepper. Place in the air fryer. Add to the air fryer bacon rashers, black pudding, and sausages. Slice tomatoes in half and season the top with salt and pepper.

Close the air fryer basket, making sure first that there is room for each of the breakfast items to cook. Then cook for 10 minutes at 180c/360f. Though at the 5-minute interval stir your eggs with a fork.

When the air fryer beeps, check to make sure the eggs are scrambled and remove the scrambled eggs with a kitchen glove or kitchen tongs. Replace the ramekin space with a ramekin of cold baked beans. Cook for a further 5 minutes at the same temperature.

When it beeps load your English breakfast ingredients onto a plate and enjoy.

Nutrition

Calories: 1496kcal | Carbohydrates: 22g | Protein: 70g | Fat: 124g | Saturated Fat: 42g | Cholesterol: 463mg | Sodium: 3005mg | Potassium: 1564mg | Fiber: 6g | Sugar: 4g | Vitamin A: 1579IU | Vitamin C: 21mg | Calcium: 117mg | Iron: 6mg

Air Fryer Bacon And Egg Toast

Prep Time: 1 Minute

Cook Time: 9 Minutes

Total Time: 10 Minutes

Ingredients

- Butter (if desired)
- 1 slice of bread
- 1 slice of bacon 1 egg
- Salt & pepper to taste

Directions

Butter a slice of bread and place it in the air fryer. Add a slice of bacon around the top of the bread.

Add an egg in the middle.

Close the air fryer and cook for 9 minutes at 340 degrees, or until the desired doneness. Salt & pepper to taste. Enjoy!

Nutritional Value

Calories:178Kcal|Totalfat:15g|Saturatedfat:8g|Transfat:0g|Cholesterol:194mg|Sodium: 193mg|Carbohydrates: 2g|Sugar: 1g|Protein: 5g| Iron: 0.8mg| Calcium: 25mg

How To Make Bacon In Your Air Fryer

Prep Time: 5 minutes

Cook Time: 10 minutes

Ingredients:

- Basic Air Fryer Bacon
- 4 pieces of thick-cut bacon
- 2 eggs
- 1 tablespoon butter
- 2 croissants sliced
- 1/2 cup ketchup
- 2 tablespoons apple cider vinegar
- 1 tablespoon molasses
- 1 tablespoon brown sugar
- 1/4 teaspoon mustard powder
- 1/4 teaspoon onion powder
- 1/2 tablespoon Worcestershire sauce
- 1/4 teaspoon liquid smoke

Instructions:

Basic Air Fryer Bacon

Preheat your Air fryer to 200 degrees C (or 390 degrees F) Lay the bacon strips of your choice flat on the Air fryer tray. Cook for 4-5 minutes, then flip the bacon.

Cook for another 4-5 minutes until the desired doneness is reached. Air Fryer Bacon With BBQ Sauce Croissants

Preheat your Air fryer to 200 degrees C (or 390 degrees F)

Whisk together in a small saucepan the ketchup, apple cider vinegar, molasses, brown sugar, mustard powder, onion powder, Worcestershire sauce, and liquid smoke. Place on medium heat and bring to a simmer, cooking until the sauce thickens slightly.

Lay the bacon flat on the Airfryer tray and brush with BBQ sauce. Cook for 4-5 minutes, then flip the bacon and brush the other side of the bacon with sauce. Cook for an additional 5 minutes or until the desired doneness is reached.

Place the croissants into your toaster and toast lightly.

Melt the butter in a medium-sized frying pan and fry the eggs until they reach your desired doneness. (over-easy is best).

Place an egg on the bottom of one croissant, followed by two bacon slices and the croissant top. Repeat with the other croissant.

Serve and enjoy!

Nutrition Information

Calories: 656kcal, Carbohydrates: 57g, Protein: 16g, Fat: 39g, Saturated Fat: 17g, Cholesterol: 246mg, Sodium: 1262mg, Potassium: 584mg, Fiber: 1g, Sugar: 33g, Vitamin A: 1145IU, Vitamin C: 3mg, Calcium: 76mg, Iron: 3mg

Air Fryer Bacon

Prep Time: 2 Minutes

Cook Time: 10 Minutes

Total Time: 12 Minutes

Ingredients

- 8 ounces bacon
- about 8 strips Water

Instructions

Preheat the air fryer at 350F for about 5 minutes.

Pour ¼ cup of water into the bottom of the air fryer to minimize smoke. Make sure the water is not touching the basket or bacon. (You can also place a layer of bread in the bottom of the air fryer.)

Place bacon in a single layer into the preheated air fryer basket. Feel free to cut bacon strips in half or even in thirds to make it fit nicely.

Cook for 8 to 10 minutes for thinner bacon and 12 to 15 minutes for thicker cut bacon.

Nutrition

Calories: 236kcal | Carbohydrates: 1g | Protein: 7g | Fat: 23g | Saturated Fat: 8g | Cholesterol: 37mg | Sodium: 375mg | Potassium: 112mg | Vitamin A: 21IU | Calcium: 3mg | Iron: 1mg

Air Fryer Egg Cups

Prep Time: 5 minutes

Cook Time: 12 minutes

Total Time: 17 minutes

Yield: 8

Ingredients

- 6 large eggs
- 1/2 cup of heavy cream (use low-fat milk for WW)
- 1/2 cup of cheddar
- 1/2 pound of breakfast sausage
- 1 tsp of olive oil
- 1 tsp of garlic
- 2 cups of spinach

Instructions

Heat a nonstick skillet to medium-low.

Add ground breakfast sausage and cook for 12-16 minutes or until cooked through and browned. Crumble the sausage with a wooden spoon or cooking utensil of choice.

Remove the breakfast sausage from the skillet. Let the sausage cool.

Add 1 tsp of olive oil and garlic to the skillet. Cook until the garlic is fragrant and Add the spinach to the skillet and cover; allow to cook 5 minutes. Take the spinach out of the pan let it cool as you did with the sausage.

In a medium bowl add the eggs and milk and whisk until combined. Fold in the cheddar, breakfast sausage, and spinach.

Place the silicone muffin cups into the air fryer basket and set the temperature to 300 degrees. Fill the cups with the egg mixture (do not overfill). I used a measuring cup to fill the muffin cups.

Set the air fryer time to 12 minutes.

I had egg mixture left over after only cooking six egg cups at a time. My air fryer basket only fit 6 muffin cups in there without overflowing. Will have to cook in batches if there is any leftover.

Nutrition Value

Calories:230|Sugar:1g|Fat:19g|Sat Fat: 7g|Unsaturated Fat: 4g|Carbohydrates: 4g| Fiber: 0g| Protein: 10g

Air Fryer Quiche

Yield: makes 1

Prep time: 10 minutes Cook time: 10 minutes

Total time: 20 minutes

Ingredients

- 1 egg
- 3-4 tbsp (45ml-60ml) of heavy cream
- 4-5 tiny broccoli florets
- 1 tbsp (15ml) finely grated cheddar cheese

Instructions

Whisk together egg and cream. Lightly grease a 5" (13cm) ceramic quiche dish. Distribute broccoli florets on the bottom. Pour in the egg mixture. Top with grated cheddar cheese.

Air fry at 325F (162C) for 10 minutes.

More Air Fryer Quiche Fillings:

Tomato and Mozzarella. Garnish with fresh basil Spinach and Cheese

Cooked bacon and Cheddar Mushroom and Thyme Smoked Salmon and Dill

Goat Cheese and Crispy Leeks (cook leeks first in a skillet with olive oil until crispy)

Nutrition Information

Calories: 656| Total Fat: 58g| Saturated Fat: 34g| Trans Fat: 2g| Unsaturated Fat: 19g| Cholesterol: 349mg| Sodium: 364mg| Carbohydrates: 18g| Fiber: 6g| Sugar: 6g| Protein: 21g

Vegan Air Fryer Breakfast Potatoes

Cook Time: 40 minutes

Total Time: 40 minutes

Ingredients

- 3 lb potatoes, diced
- 2 bell peppers, any color, diced
- 1 onion, diced
- 15 oz mushrooms, diced
- 1 1/2 cups or 1-14 oz can black beans, drained
- Lemon Miso Tahini Sauce, optional
- Spinach and avocado for serving, optional

Instructions

IF AIR FRYING: Add potatoes to the air fryer basket. Cook 20 minutes at 400 degrees F (or 205 degrees C), shaking basket frequently.

Add beans and vegetables and cook 10 - 15 more minutes until potatoes are soft or crispy, according to preference.

IF BAKING: Spread potatoes out on a lined baking tray and bake for 25-30 minutes in a 425 degree F (218 degrees C) oven.

Remove the tray and flip the potatoes. Add your veggies and beans and stir. Put the tray back in the oven for 15-20 more minutes, until the potatoes have started to get crispy and lightly golden brown and until all the veggies have cooked.

Make the lemon miso tahini sauce by mixing the ingredients in a bowl and thinning the sauce with water if needed.

Add to a bowl with spinach and whatever else you like (this would be a great complement to tofu scramble, for instance). Top with sauce mixture and enjoy!

Refrigerate leftovers in an airtight container for up to 5 days. Recommended reheating in the oven, skillet, or air fryer to retain crispiness.

Nutritional Value

Calories: 164 Total Fat: 0.5g Sodium: 200.5g

Total carbohydrate: 34.7g Sugar: 4g

Protein: 7.2g

Fried Eggs For The Air Fryer

Prep Time: 1 Minute

Cook Time: 8 Minutes

Total Time: 9 Minutes

Ingredients

- 2 Large Eggs
- 2 Tablespoons Butter
- Salt And Pepper

Instructions

Add a small aluminum pan to the basket of an air fryer.

Add the butter and heat at 350 degrees to melt (approximately 1 minute) Crack both eggs into the aluminum pan.

Return to the air fryer and cook at 325-degrees until your desired doneness.

Nutrition Information

Calories: 363 Total Fat: 33g Saturated Fat: 18g

Cholesterol: 482mg Sodium: 361mg Carbohydrates: 1g Sugar: 1g

Protein: 14g

Turkey Breakfast Sausage - Air Fryer Or Oven Method

Prep Time: 5 Minutes

Cook Time: 13 Minutes

Total Time: 18 Minutes

Ingredients

- 1 pound ground turkey
- 1 teaspoon kosher salt
- ½ teaspoon black pepper
- 1 teaspoon fennel seed
- ½ teaspoon ground sage
- ½ teaspoon smoked paprika 3/4 teaspoon garlic powder
- 1/8 teaspoon red pepper flakes (or to taste)

Instructions

Place all the ingredients in a medium bowl and mix well to combine.

Wet hands with water and form the ground turkey mixture into 12-13 small patties (approximately 1½ tablespoons, each).

Place the patties on an air fryer baking sheet and cook for 12-13 minutes at 350-degrees (or until an instant-read thermometer reached 165-degrees when inserted into the center of a sausage.

Nutrition Information

Calories: 91 Total Fat: 6g Saturated Fat: 2g

Unsaturated Fat: 4g Cholesterol: 37mg Sodium: 193mg Protein: 9g

Dry Rub Skirt Steak Sandwiches

Prep Time: 10 Minutes

Cook Time: 15 Minutes

Inactive Time: 30 Minutes

Total Time: 55 Minutes

Ingredients

For The Dry Rub

- 3 tablespoons ground coriander
- 3 tablespoons smoked paprika
- 3 tablespoons ground smoked cumin
- 1 teaspoon allspice
- 1½ tablespoons ground cinnamon
- 2 tablespoons dried oregano
- 1½ tablespoons dry mustard
- 3 tablespoons salt
- 1½ tablespoons black pepper
- 2 tablespoons garlic powder
- 4 tablespoons brown sugar

For the sandwich

- 2 beef skirt steaks

- 1 tablespoon canola oil
- 3 green bell peppers, seeded and sliced
- 2 large sweet onions, peeled and sliced
- ½ teaspoon salt
- ¼ teaspoon pepper
- 8 crusty rolls
- 1½ cup beef broth for dipping, optional hot sauce, optional

Instructions

In a large bowl with a lid, mix all the ingredients for the dry rub until well combined.

Place the meat on the baking sheet and liberally sprinkle the dry rub on both sides of the meat and rub it in lightly.

Allow the meat to sit for approximately 30 minutes.

Meanwhile, heat a large skillet to medium, add the canola oil and the sliced peppers and onions.

Sautee the green peppers and onions with ½ teaspoon salt and ¼ pepper until they softened and cooked through. Remove from heat and keep warm.

Place the steaks on a hot grill and cook for approximately 5 minutes per side.

Remove the cooked steaks from the grill and allow them to sit, covered with aluminum foil, for at least 10 minutes.

Slice the meat across the grain in thin slices.

To serve pile the sliced beef onto crusty rolls and top with the sauteed peppers and onions.

Spoon (or dip) the beef stock over the prepared sandwiches and a few shakes of hot sauce if desired. Serve hot!

Nutrition Information

Calories: 399 Total Fat: 17g Saturated Fat: 5g Trans Fat: 0g

Unsaturated Fat: 10g Cholesterol: 64mg Sodium: 3218mg Carbohydrates: 37g Fiber: 7g

Sugar: 13g Protein: 27g

Air Fryer Mini Breakfast Burritos

Prep Time: 15 mins

Cook Time: 30 mins

Total Time: 45 mins

Ingredients

- ¼ cup Mexican-style chorizo 1 tablespoon bacon grease
- ½ cup diced potatoes
- 2 tablespoons chopped onion 1 serrano pepper, chopped
- 2 large eggs
- Salt and ground black pepper to taste 4 (8 inches) flour tortillas
- Avocado oil cooking spray

Instructions

Cook chorizo in a large skillet over medium-high heat, stirring frequently until sausage turns a dark red, 6 to 8 minutes. Remove from the skillet and set aside.

Melt bacon grease in the same skillet over medium-high heat. Add diced potatoes and cook, stirring occasionally, 8 to 10 minutes. Add onion and serrano pepper and continue cooking and stirring until potatoes are fork-tender, onion is translucent, and serrano pepper is soft, 2 to 6 minutes. Add eggs and chorizo; stir until cooked and completely incorporated into potato mixture, about 5 minutes. Season with salt and pepper.

Meanwhile, heat tortillas in a large skillet or directly on the grates of a gas stove until soft and pliable. Place 1/3 cup chorizo mixture down the center of each tortilla. Fold top and bottom of tortillas over the filling, then roll each into a burrito shape. Mist with cooking spray and place in the basket of an air fryer.

Air fry at 400 degrees F (200 degrees C) for 4 to 6 minutes. Flip each burrito over, mist with cooking spray, and air fry until lightly browned, 2 to 4 minutes more.

Nutritional Value

Calories: 253.8 Protein: 8.3g Carbohydrates: 31.4g Dietary Fiber: 2.2g Sugars: 0.6g

Fat: 10.4g Saturated Fat: 3.3g

Cholesterol: 98.1mg Vitamin B6: 0.1mg Vitamin C: 4.9mg Folate: 76.5mcg Calcium: 36.1mg Iron: 2.3mg Magnesium: 21.4mg Potassium: 198.4mg Sodium: 298.2mg

Air Fryer Churros

Prep Time: 5 mins

Cook Time: 15 mins

Additional Time: 5 mins

Total Time: 25 mins

Ingredients

- ¼ cup butter
- ½ cup milk 1 pinch salt
- ½ cup all-purpose flour
- 2 eggs
- ¼ cup white sugar
- ½ teaspoon ground cinnamon

Instructions

Melt butter in a saucepan over medium-high heat. Pour in milk and add salt. Lower heat to medium and bring to a boil, continuously stirring with a wooden spoon. Quickly add flour all at once. Keep stirring until the dough comes together.

Remove from heat and let cool for 5 to 7 minutes. Mix in eggs with the wooden spoon until the pastry comes together. Spoon dough into a pastry bag fitted with a large star tip. Pipe dough into strips straight into the air fryer basket.

Air fry churros at 340 degrees F (175 degrees C) for 5 minutes.

Meanwhile, combine sugar and cinnamon in a small bowl and pour onto a shallow plate. Remove fried churros from the air fryer and roll in the cinnamon-sugar mixture.

Nutrition Facts

Protein: 3.9g Carbohydrates: 17.5g

Dietary Fiber: 0.4g Sugars: 9.4g

Fat: 9.8g

Saturated Fat: 5.6g Cholesterol: 84mg Vitamin A Iu: 356.5IU Niacin Equivalents: 1.5mg Folate: 28.2mcg

Calcium: 38.5mg Iron: 0.8mg Magnesium: 6.8mg Potassium: 67.2mg Sodium: 112.2mg Thiamin: 0.1mg

Calories From Fat: 88.5

Lightning Source UK Ltd.
Milton Keynes UK
UKHW020643300421
382900UK00010B/362